1986

Congress and the Media: The Ethical Connection

INSTITUTE OF
SOCIETY, ETHICS AND
THE LIFE
SCIENCES

THE HASTINGS CENTER

Congress and the Media: The Ethical Connection

By *DANIEL CALLAHAN, WILLIAM GREEN, BRUCE JENNINGS, and MARTIN LINSKY*

The Hastings Center
Institute of Society, Ethics and the Life Sciences
360 Broadway
Hastings-on-Hudson, New York 10706

Printed in the United States of America

Contents

Foreword

The genesis of this essay dates back to the summer and fall of 1980. The Hastings Center was contacted by the staff of the Senate Select Committee on Ethics to consult with them in their study of possible revisions to the Senate Code of Official Conduct. The Senate code, like its counterpart in the House, is a technical, legalistic document that bears the heavy mark, not only of the legislative hands who composed it, but also of the mode of thinking about legislative ethics dominant in congressional discussions in recent years. That mode of thinking is preoccupied with the use of office for personal gain and financial conflict of interest—and thus the Senate code regulates such things as the receipt of gifts and honoraria, financial disclosure, the use of the frank for mass mailings, and the like. These are important matters, to be sure, but the code fails to provide any ethical foundations or rationale for its own regulations and prohibitions, and it is strangely silent on numerous ethically significant dimensions of a legislator's power and role.

We readily perceived these philosophical problems with the code, both because the area of legislative ethics was new to us so we were not habituated to established approaches to these problems, and because we had seen many of the same problems arise in other professions where discussions of ethical issues and codes have evolved from narrowly financial questions—fee splitting in medicine, for example—to much broader ethical concerns. We saw no good reason why the study of legislative ethics should not evolve and develop in the same way, and our subsequent work has attempted to promote that evolution.

In our meetings with senators and ethics committee staff members we gained a sense of the practical problems they had with regulating the ethical conduct of legislators and enforcing the code. It was then that we first realized how significant was the effect of the media in the process of internal ethics regulation in Congress and in shaping legislators' attitudes toward that process.

Anxiety about media coverage of legislative ethics runs high among Senate and House members. They feel caught in a no-win situation. However much some congressmen might like to, they believe that they cannot loosen the formal ethics regulations of the post-Watergate era, even those that appear to be inefficient and counterproductive; to do so would be interpreted as a retreat from ethics. The press, congressional staff members confidently assured us, would have a field day with that. On the other hand, members of Congress are exceedingly wary about any suggestion to broaden the scope of legislative ethics. When we asked why the code could not include, for instance, an assertion of a legislator's ethical responsibility to Congress as an institution, or why in the Senate the use of the filibuster was not as much an ethical issue as the use of the frank, we were told that extending the concept of ethics in this way would have, as Senator Howell Heflin put it, a "chilling effect" on legislative behavior. Ethics is a lightning rod for critical media coverage as well as for attacks by political opponents. Legislators do not want to acknowledge the subtle and nuanced ethical aspects of the political and tactical decisions they make, not so much because they do not see that these ethical aspects exist, but because they have little confidence that the press can or will convey the subtlety.

Thus we found legislators, from their vantage point at least, caught in a trap. They cannot seem to fine-tune the regulations covering those aspects of legislative life that have been defined as ethical issues, and they are most hesitant to invite a more far-reaching public discussion of other aspects of legislative life that do, in fact, involve ethical issues but have not been defined as such. This bind is not simply one legislators have created for themselves. It is, in part, a function of the relationship between legislators and the press, and of the perceptions legislators have of the way the press reports on congressional ethics and legislative affairs generally. There is a measure of paranoia in these perceptions, to be sure. But there is a measure of truth in them as well. Today, nearly five years and many hours of meetings and hearings later, the Senate Ethics Committee is still on hold in the process of revising the Senate code.

Intrigued by our experience in consulting with the Senate committee—and surprised by the fact that almost no philosophical or scholarly work had been done on legislative ethics—in 1981 we began a new research project at the Center designed to explore the theoretical foundations of legislative ethics and the ethics of representation. Supported by a grant from the Ford Foundation, we assembled a task force comprised of congressmen and state legislators, political scientists, philosophers, and other scholars. This group met several times over the course of three years to discuss the ethical obligations of legislative representatives in a democracy and the implications of recent changes that have occurred both within legislatures and in the electoral system. In this project we explored three basic principles—autonomy, accountability, and responsibility—that seemed to define the scope of legislative ethics. In the light of these principles we discussed the ethical problems and dilemmas created by the decentralization of power in legislatures, the rise of legislative entrepreneurialism, the growing influence of Political Action Committees, and the like. Our initial sense of the importance of the media in shaping public understanding of legislative ethics—and in fostering a climate of information and ideas that would encourage legislators to fulfill their ethical obligations—was reinforced in these discussions. This project recently concluded with the publication of its final report, *The Ethics of Legislative Life* (Hastings-on-Hudson: The Hastings Center, 1985). A companion volume of essays commissioned for the project, Bruce Jennings and Daniel Callahan, eds., *Representation and Responsibility: Exploring Legislative Ethics,* will be published later this year by Plenum Press.

As our studies progressed, it became apparent that a separate project would be necessary to do full justice to the questions raised by the role of the media in the ethics of legislative life. Accordingly, in 1983, with support from the John and Mary R. Markle Foundation, we began a second research project on Legislative Ethics and the Media. The task force assembled for this project was made up of journalists representing various specialties and perspectives within the media as well as legislators, congressional staff members, and academic experts. We supplemented our project group meetings with a number of lengthy interviews to solicit the views of congressmen and journalists who could not attend those meetings. (A list of project participants and those interviewed is included at the end of this volume.)

Initially, we planned to concentrate exclusively on media coverage of ethical issues in Congress. But our inquiry soon expanded as it became apparent that this was but one aspect of a much broader relationship between all legislatures and the press, a relationship that raises as many questions about the professional ethical obligations of legislative journalists as it does about the ethical obligations of federal and state legislators.

The essay presented here, coauthored by ourselves and by William Green and Martin Linsky, who served as participants and consultants in our task force, is an outgrowth of the Legislative Ethics and the Media Project. While the argument of this essay is our own, and does not reflect a consensus reached by our project task force, it does build upon the project meetings and interviews to a large extent.

Congress and the Media: The Ethical Connection is meant to lay a groundwork for what we hope will be an enhanced dialogue among legislators and journalists in the future. Our aim is to pursue the notion that the ethics of representation provides a common framework for a fresh understanding of the moral obligations of journalists and legislators. Since this is an essay intended to begin a conversation, rather than a research monograph offering a definitive treatment of its subject, we have deliberately kept footnotes and other scholarly accoutrements to a minimum. Readers wishing to pursue further the issues we raise may consult the references provided in the select bibliography.

We wish to thank the John and Mary R. Markle Foundation for the support which made the Hastings Center project and this study possible; and Deborah Wadsworth, formerly a Program Officer with the Foundation, for her initial encouragement and support. John Saxon gave us the benefit of his ideas and experience throughout the project and helped us arrange and conduct several interviews. We would like to thank most heartily as well all those who took part in our project meetings and those who agreed to be interviewed. They cannot be held responsible for the errors of fact or judgment that may appear in this essay. But we hope they will be given credit for whatever insight the essay may contain.

Finally, Mary Gualandi deserves special praise for her skillful and good-natured assistance in typing and retyping the manuscript of this essay.

DANIEL CALLAHAN   BRUCE JENNINGS
Project Co-Directors

I. Introduction

Representation and the Press

In an address to the American Society of Newspaper Editors in 1982, Michael O'Neill, former editor of the *New York Daily News*, provocatively suggested that in pursuing its negative role as a critic of governmental activities, the press* had lost sight of its equally important positive role as a constructive enabling force in the democratic process. "No longer do we look on government only with the healthy skepticism required by professional tradition," he maintained. "Now we have a hard, intensively adversarial attitude. We treat the government as the enemy—and government officials as convenient targets for attack-and-destroy missions."[1] O'Neill's comments reflect a growing sentiment among some within and outside professional journalism that the pendulum has swung too far in the direction of adversarialism and an appetite for political scandal in the post-Watergate era.

Not surprisingly, this claim provoked considerable controversy in the profession. Many journalists questioned the accuracy of his emphasis on the adversarial nature of contemporary political reporting. Some went further and held that far from being too quarrelsome and critical, the press was not critical enough. When asked by the Poynter Institute for Media Studies to comment on O'Neill's speech, Benjamin Bradlee, executive editor of the *Washington Post*, said: "Mike talks about the press' harshly adversarial posture toward government. Baloney. I'd like to talk about the selling of the presidency, the manipulation of the public, where the press is a captive, if not willing, victim."[2]

Our research indicates that O'Neill's portrait of an excessively adversarial press is indeed overdrawn. But it is unfortunate that so much of the ensuing debate focused on that theme, because it has obscured another, much more fundamental aspect of O'Neill's

---

*In this essay we use the terms "press" and "media" interchangeably. Those specific facets of the print and electronic media being referred to at various points in our discussion will be clear from the context.

argument; namely, the effect the media have on the continued viability of democratic institutions.

Concern about the destructive effects of media coverage on public confidence in government has recently been expressed in the writings of many political scientists and former public officials. Disillusioned by the record of the Carter administration and the Congress in the late 1970s, they believe that governmental institutions have become so fragmented by conflicting social pressures and so stymied by a lack of effective leadership that they are unable to make the hard decisions and policy choices required to solve urgent social problems.[3] His thinking influenced to some degree by this analysis, and facing the prospect of an impending crisis of democratic governance, O'Neill wondered aloud whether the time had come for the profession of journalism to rethink its social responsibilities and its role as a key actor in the democratic process:

> The mass media, especially television, are not only changing the way government is covered but the way it functions. The crucial relationship between the people and their elected representatives—the very core of our political system—has been altered fundamentally. . . . The media have . . . made a considerable contribution to the disarray in government and therefore have an obligation to help set matters straight. Or at least improve them. The corollary of increased power is increased responsibility. The press cannot stand apart, as if it were not an interested party, not to say participant, in the democratic process.[4]

This notion of the media's democratic responsibilities, and not the subsidiary issue of adversarialism, poses the basic questions with which we shall be concerned. Is contemporary political journalism serving the needs of a healthy democracy well? What is the proper scope of the media's responsibility here, and how can that responsibility be fulfilled in practice? What relationship should obtain between those who hold political power and authority and the Fourth Estate? Is the press too critical or too compliant? Is the political role of the media limited to providing a negative check on the abuse of power by elected representatives, or can the press also positively enhance the ability of conscientious officials to fulfill their ethical obligations and their public trust?

In this essay we propose to examine these and related questions by focusing on the relationship between the media and Congress, rather than the executive branch or government as a whole. And our special concern will be the "ethical connection" between Congress and the media, namely, how the ethical practice of congressional journalism can enhance—and, indeed, is essential to—the ethical practice of congressional representation.

In the meetings and interviews we conducted with legislators, congressional staff, and journalists as background for this study, we discovered that few on either side felt that "adversarialism" is an accurate characterization of the relationship between Congress and the press. At the same time, neither side believed that adversarialism or its opposite—uncritical deference and cooperation—are adequate notions to capture the ethical dimension of that relationship: how Congress and the press as institutions, and how legislators and journalists as individuals *should* interact in a democratic system.

But if neither adversarialism nor its opposite is appropriate, what conception does capture the relationship between Congress and the media as it is and as it should be? We suggest that the appropriate conception is to be found in the notion of representation. The basic thesis of this study can be stated as follows: *Even though they occupy significantly different positions, have different institutional resources at their disposal, and function under different kinds of public expectations and demands, legislators and journalists are both essential actors in the overall process of democratic representation as it has evolved in the United States. For this reason, the moral duties of congressional journalists and legislators are not at odds, but flow from the same source. Both have parallel moral obligations that derive from the ethics of representation.*

It has become common to think of the congressional media as outside the legislative process, as external observers who simply describe and explain what legislators do. Yet, as our study progressed it became clear that this image is misleading. The media are an indispensable element in the broader pattern of institutionalized political representation. This is true, not merely because the press serves as the principal medium for informing constituents about the activities of legislators, but for two additional reasons as well. First, in practical and important ways, what the press reports, and how the press reports it, affects the capacity and incentives of individual legislators to function as ethically responsible representatives, and affects the capacity of Congress to function effectively as a representational institution. Second, the various mechanisms designed by the legislature to promote the ethically responsible use of its authority, to deter misconduct, and to correct abuses are dependent upon the media for their effectiveness and success. Codes of ethics, financial disclosure requirements, and campaign finance regulations require, in varying degrees, timely, accurate, and well-informed press coverage if they are to work as they were intended to.

In short, while journalists may seem to be merely outsiders and spectators to the process of representation, in very real and important ways they are not outsiders at all but de facto participants. As such, they and the press as an institution bear a share of the ethical burden and responsibility for the success or the failure of the process of representation in fulfilling its proper democratic mission.

In the years ahead, our democratic institutions—and Congress in particular—will be faced with many serious, universally acknowledged problems: controlling the federal debt, reducing poverty and hard-core unemployment, planning for future energy needs, solving immense public health and environmental problems, modernizing industry and transportation systems, and so on. Solving these problems will pose a severe test for the viability of Congress. It will be a test of the capacity of our legislative representatives to combine enlightened leadership with popular accountability in fashioning public policies that effectively address social problems and are sufficiently balanced and equitable to command broad public support. It will also test the ability of members of Congress to increase public confidence and trust in their integrity and leadership. To do this congressmen must educate their constituents on the issues, help promote a realistic understanding of and expectations about the workings of Congress as an institution, and earn public confidence by demonstrating a high level of ethical integrity. In a sense, the second of these tests is the more important because it holds the key to meeting the first successfully.

Legitimate democratic representation requires three important moral virtues, virtues necessary both to carry out effectively the role of representation, and to convey to the general public an image of rectitude and probity. Legislators should be morally autonomous agents whose decisions are based on rational, informed, unbiased, and uncoerced judgments. Legislators should be accountable and responsive to constituents' interests, while at the same time informing and educating constituents about what reasonably can be accomplished. And finally, legislators should act in ways that help sustain or improve systems of representation and lawmaking that are responsive to the legitimate interests of all citizens and to the common good of the nation as a whole. The ethical duties that follow these fundamental requirements of legitimate democratic representation are based on what we shall call the principles of autonomy, accountability, and responsibility. These principles comprise a generic framework for the ethics of representation. They define the basic obligations of all those who play a significant role in the representational process, and therefore apply both to legislators and to congressional journalists as well.

The dynamics of political representation turn largely on public perception and trust. When lawmakers enjoy trust, they have the latitude to act as leaders or statesmen, exercising their own informed judgment about how the interests both of their constituents and the nation can be served. When necessary, they can take unpopular stands without undue risk that the voters will reject their leadership at the next election. When the underlying public trust is lacking, however, this healthy process of representing by leading, and leading by representing, falters. When public suspicion and cynicism about legislative corruption takes hold, to say nothing of apathy among the majority of a legislator's constituents, the legislator loses the option of appealing to a broad audience. At best, it becomes difficult to withstand a narrow, focused, and often intense opposition of particular interest groups.

The question is: how can legislators be motivated to perform their function and use their authority ethically so as to increase the public confidence upon which their ability to govern effectively depends? Clearly, much of the burden here must fall on legislators themselves—on their own courage, honesty, and integrity; on their ability to understand the ethical obligations of their role, to weigh the moral significance of their actions, and to resolve the myriad ethical dilemmas they face. It will depend also on their political skills in building support among their constituents and working effectively within the legislative process; and on their own conscience and sense of personal dedication to the high standards of public service.

But it is equally clear that individual legislators, no matter how skilled and how dedicated, cannot do this alone. They require institutional support from the legislature itself, and from legislative leaders. They require support from reasonably well-informed and fair-minded constituents. Most critically, they require support from other important social, political, and governmental institutions whose activities influence the nexus of relationships between legislators and constituents, other public officials, and other actors in the legislative process, and among legislators themselves. Foremost among those institutions that influence this representational nexus are the media.

Contemporary news organizations form a crucial link in the process of political representation in the United States, and future challenges to the viability of representative government are challenges for the media as much as they are challenges for Congress or for individual legislators.

The congressional journalist is the "eyes and ears" of the

absent citizenry in Washington. Their "constituents" are their readers, listeners, and viewers. Journalists provide a kind of supplemental representation for these people, sometimes confirming and sometimes challenging the primary representation performed by elected legislators. As unelected representatives, journalists have their own special obligations to fulfill. We believe that these obligations, like the concomitant ethical obligations of legislators, derive from the principles of autonomy, accountability, and responsibility.

Dilemmas in Covering Legislative Ethics

To get an initial sense of the connection between the representational duties of journalists and those of legislators, consider three recent cases: the coverage of financial disclosure information, the coverage of congressional salary increases, and the coverage of the 1982 House page scandal.

Since 1977 congressmen have been required to disclose publicly the sources and amount of their personal and family income on an annual basis.[5] The main purpose of these financial disclosure regulations is to afford voters a clearer sense of the possible influences on the judgments and behavior of representatives. It was meant to be a means, in particular, of judging the autonomy of legislators.

In practice, however, the effectiveness of these laws has rested almost entirely upon the press in making available to the public the results of financial disclosure. While it is of course perfectly possible for a citizen to go to Washington (or the state capitol where they are also filed) and look at the pertinent forms, it would in fact require a great deal of energy and dedication on the part of the citizen to do that. Moreover, the information on the forms is by no means self-explanatory; simply trying to understand the significance of various holdings and financial transactions is a difficult and time-consuming task. Thus, from the outset, the media were seen to be essential in making the laws work, both by transmitting to the public the information in the disclosure forms and by interpreting the meaning of that information in terms of the possible unethical conflicts of interest it revealed. Financial disclosure simply cannot function but for a role played by the media, and cannot function well unless they play that role responsibly. On the whole press coverage has not done much to make disclosure an effective deterrent to conflicts of interest.

Another issue in which press coverage has implications for congressional ethics is pay raises. Members of Congress are in an unusual position: very few of us are required to set our own salaries, to do so in public view, and explain and justify the decision to hundreds of thousands of people who, collectively, can throw us out of our jobs. The way the pay-raise issue is presented to the public is therefore a matter of special importance for the legislator.

Over the years, legislators have come to distrust the press in this area. They regard voting for a pay raise as a politically dangerous act, whether or not it is justified on its merits. Balanced press coverage of this issue, they believe, is rare. Many journalists do not understand or sympathize with arguments in favor of increasing congressional salaries; even when personal bias plays no role in shaping coverage, the reigning conventions of what constitutes a "good story" tend to emphasize the dramatic, rhetorical arguments against a pay increase. Charges that legislators are self-serving, greedy, and hypocritical make good copy, and it is easy for reporters to find individual legislators who are ready to make those charges, because it is politically beneficial back home to do so. Thus a convergence of the journalistic priorities of some reporters and the political priorities of some legislators all too often seems to work against an open, rational public discussion of congressional compensation. As a result, many members of Congress believe themselves faced with a Hobson's choice either of forgoing reasonable salary increases or trying to slip them through with a minimum of publicity.

Too often, Congress has taken the latter route. Pay raises have been tacked onto other bills as ad hoc amendments, pushed through in the rush of business at the end of a session, or otherwise enacted without adequate discussion within the Congress or with the public. Naturally, these tactics have fueled the cycle of mistrust between the press and Congress. The result is a picture presented to the public in which voting against a pay raise is understood to be the ethical path for legislators to take, and in which the image of Congress as an institution is tarnished. Journalists do not intentionally cause this result; they simply act out one part of a larger drama. However, the press must ultimately assume responsibility for its decisions about how much coverage to give to the issue, how much to play along with those who exploit the issue for their own grandstanding, and how to frame it for the public.

The third example is that of the 1982 House page scandal, allegedly involving numerous House members in sexual and drug abuses with pages—high school students temporarily employed by the House as legislative messengers.[6] For several years House pages had been living on their own in Washington without adequate supervision by House officials responsible for the page program. In 1982 many rumors were circulating on Capitol Hill concerning wild parties, drug trafficking, and alcohol abuse among some pages. Little attention was paid to these rumors until one CBS correspondent met with two teenage pages who made allegations about the involvement of House members in homosexual affairs. With their faces shielded, these teenagers were interviewed in a CBS news broadcast on June 30, 1982. This dramatic broadcast led to widespread coverage of the allegations throughout the country. Eventually, the teenagers recanted their stories, and subsequent congressional and FBI investigations proved that the charges were unfounded. But the public reputation of the Congress undoubtedly suffered in this affair. As usual, the general public was more aware of the fact that a scandal was alleged than that it was subsequently shown to be unfounded.

This incident is especially troubling because it demonstrates the damaging impact a single correspondent can have when careful journalistic practices are not followed and when a news organization fails to exercise appropriate editorial restraint. In this case, the desire to uncover a major scandal apparently led the correspondent to elicit sensational charges from disturbed and immature sources and then to air the story without adequate investigation or corroboration. An important and accurate story that might have been brought to public attention—the failure of the House to supervise adequately the living arrangements and conduct of pages after hours—was overlooked, while a much more lurid, but false, scandal was zealously pursued.

These cases are, admittedly, rather extreme examples of the way press coverage either affects the workings of legislative ethics regulation or inadvertently fuels public mistrust and misunderstanding of Congress as an institution. But even in less extreme cases the press finds it difficult to cover the more subtle aspects of legislative ethics.

As is typically the case with most matters of ethics, there is often a gap between the ideals that are to be sought and the ethical principles upon which they rest, and the actual implementation of those values in the day-to-day life of legislators. There is a wide range of ambiguous situations where the proper application of the moral principles is by no means clear, and where the legislator has also to cope with public perceptions of his or her role. In many instances the media can enhance the ability of individual legislators to fulfill their ethical obligation and the capacity of legislatures to enforce ethical standards of conduct. The media provide a positive goad to legislators and turn a healthy searchlight on their behavior. But the power of the media also creates considerable nervousness among legislators, which in turn gives them an inclination to evade accountability and to avoid responsibility.

Among legislators, it is widely believed that the media have a tendency to emphasize or sensationalize suggestions of impropriety where none really exists. Legislators also feel that journalists, for the sake of a "good story," jump to premature conclusions before they have all the facts; that they tend to err on the side of criticism rather than giving the benefit of doubt; that they have generally cynical and hostile attitudes toward legislative politics; and that they have a penchant for scandal, rather than a genuine desire to help citizens understand the full range of complex ethical issues legislators face.

Allegations of impropriety often surface in the press. Journalists have good sources and well-honed investigative techniques. Sometimes charges are taken to the media because those with a grievance know that this is one way to ensure that their charges will not be ignored. Legislators are often put in the difficult position of having to respond to issues they learn about from news coverage. If they respond defensively or do not respond at all, they appear to be hiding something. Sometimes they are and sometimes they aren't; but either way first impressions can cause lasting damage. Inevitably, if the media gets to an issue first, it looks as if the legislature and legislative ethics committees have not been doing their proper job of self-policing. If an ethics committee is slow and deliberate about investigating an ethics violation, it appears to be dragging its feet. Ordinary citizens are left with the impression that the foxes are guarding the chicken coop.

Many legislators are also ambivalent about the proper role of the media in examining their personal and private lives. They do not want to appear to be opposing freedom of the press, or legitimate examination of their activities, but it is a significant burden of public life to have intimate details of one's private conduct relentlessly scrutinized on national television and in hometown newspapers.[7]

A further problem complicating the media's impact on legislative ethics is that the rules of procedure followed by legislative ethics committees, which are designed to ensure due process protections for the accused, seem to stand in the way of full and immediate disclosure to the public and the media. This problem is further compounded by the fact that internal disciplinary proceedings must often await the outcome of Justice Department investigations and court proceedings. From the viewpoint of the public, this again can often look like a cover-up, and it is very difficult to explain the subtle relationship between the requirements of due process and the requirements of legitimate public information.

In these and other ways, the coverage of legislative ethics exemplifies the clash of values and priorities that is built into the tension between legislators and journalists.

II. The Relationship Between Journalists and Legislators

Sweeping generalizations about the relationship between journalists and legislators are as risky as they are common. The relationship is a product of a long history and tradition and of complex traditional images of what journalists and legislators are and should be. At any given time it is shaped by the way in which legislators and journalists see themselves, by professional conventions, and by institutional constraints. It is affected by the outside forces of technological innovation, legal doctrine, and prevailing public attitudes. It is made up of hundreds of individual interactions between different journalists and different legislators, interactions shaped by personal chemistry and the vicissitudes of circumstance.

Many observers have tried in vain to characterize the relationship between journalists and legislators with a single word, such as "adversarial" or "symbiotic" or "cozy." But no single adjective can really capture the multiple, varying ways reporters and legislators deal with each other. In our interviews and meetings with journalists and legislators, however, some general themes did stand out.

The journalist-legislator relationship has undergone an important change in the last two decades. Journalists are more wary of the dangers of co-optation and a "cozy relationship"; legislators are more sophisticated about public relations techniques and are more "media conscious." Second, neither journalists nor legislators are content with the present quality of press coverage of the Congress, although there is little agreement on why there is a problem or what can be done about it. Also, much of the tension that does exist between legislators and journalists stems from legitimate but conflicting interests and roles. Yet another theme is the plurality of the press. Within the media covering Congress there are many diverse news organizations with varying missions and a wide range of concerns and attitudes. The congressional news media are plural in deed as well as in word. Finally, of all the aspects of congressional activity covered by the press, those involving congressional ethics or those that highlight the ethical dimensions of legislative service are among the most provocative to legislators and the most complicated for the press.

The Historical Context

As a historical generalization, it is misleading to speak of an adversarial tradition in American political journalism in general, and in relations between the press and the Congress in particular. To gain a better understanding of this issue, it is useful to distinguish three distinct periods of press-Congress relations.[8]

The first, between colonial times and the Civil War, was characterized by partisanship and intimacy. Newspapers unabashedly championed political causes, and when the party of their choice was in power, they actively cooperated with the government by serving as semiofficial organs of information. Most of whatever conflict did arise between the press and the Congress stemmed from differences between them over access to the floor, seating space in the galleries, and the like.

The second period stretches from the Civil War to the 1970s, and is characterized by the change in newspapers from information sources for relatively small, highly partisan audiences to mass market publications. This transformation in the newspaper business brought with it a new theory of journalistic objectivity. As much a marketing notion as an editorial principle, the notion of objectivity held that by freeing the news of partisanship and making it "objective," newspapers could turn everyone into a potential customer.

To progressive reformers and critics of the older, partisan press, the developing norm of objectivity meant that the press could be a more independent, responsible source of the information citizens in a democracy needed to hold their representatives accountable. But politicians soon adapted to the new rules of the game and learned how to turn this notion of what constituted ethical journalism to their own advantage. The possibilities of the political manipulation of the press under the guise of objectivity was not widely recognized until the 1950s and the rise of Senator Joseph McCarthy. In the wake of the McCarthy era, some journalists began to question publicly whether the spirit of objectivity was serving society well. But if McCarthyism marked the beginning of second thoughts about the norm of objectivity, Vietnam and Watergate dealt the final blows. By the early 1970s, the relationship between the press and the government in general, and Congress in particular, had entered a new phase.

The third and current phase of relations between the press and

Congress is characterized by the legitimization, although not the regular practice, of what has come to be called adversary journalism. Adversary journalism has greatly reinforced the idea, already implicit in the progressive notion of objectivity, that the press, as a surrogate for the people, has a responsibility to hold government accountable, root out wrongs, expose corruption, and help throw the rascals out of office.

Just as the press's understanding of its relationship to Congress has changed over time, so too has Congress's understanding of its relationship to the press. Congress needs the media as a means of communicating with the public and as a means of gauging public feedback and sentiment. Today virtually all congressmen assign staff members to handle press relations and to monitor news and editorial coverage in major national and district media. New telecommunications technologies and direct-mail techniques are beginning to enable legislators to establish more direct links with their constituents, but the media still "mediates" the representational relationship between legislators and constituents in decisive ways.[9]

Similarly, news organizations need Congress. Congress is the single largest source of political news and information. It is a virtual clearinghouse of nationally significant events, and the tremendous growth of federally controlled programs since World War II has also made Congress a source of regionally or locally important news for smaller papers.

In short, even in the recent atmosphere of somewhat greater adversarialism than has been typical historically, individual legislators and individual reporters must rely on one another in order to do their jobs. Legislators cultivate relationships with reporters in order to enlist them in building political support for legislative programs. Reporters depend upon individual legislators for stories because, given prevailing editorial conventions and organizational demands, no reporter can produce acceptable copy by relying on officially published documents and outside sources alone. Each party to this exceedingly complex relationship understands that the other seeks to turn the relationship to his own advantage. Both use the relationship and feel used by it. And both sense the fragility of the relationship; both learn to respect invisible lines that must not be crossed.

Criticism of Coverage

In our interviews and meetings, both legislators and journalists freely criticized coverage of Congress. Both seemed to sense that the press did not cover well the real work of the Congress: the behind-the-scenes activity, the procedural strictures that control the ebb and flow of legislation, and the consensus-building efforts that consume so much time and effort on the part of individual congressmen.

Many agreed, for example, that the press focuses too exclusively on the most visible elements of the legislative process, such as committee hearings and floor debates. What goes largely unreported are all the behind-the-scenes efforts to bargain and negotiate, to resolve differences and build consensus. As William Greider of *Rolling Stone* pointed out, if there is no fight, there is no coverage. Yet much of the activity of individual congressmen is devoted to avoiding a fight. This is not primarily because congressmen seek to avoid press coverage, but because it is in the nature of the legislative process to seek compromise and to work out differences.

And yet, by its very nature, what goes on behind the scenes is difficult to report. Members of Congress themselves do little to make it easier for journalists to cover this hidden face of the legislative process. The same pressures that push toward consensus also push toward keeping that part of the process out of the public eye. Members of Congress are unsure of public acceptance of the way they do business, at least in part because they do not have confidence in the way that this activity would be reported. Many legislators understand that a consequence of this is that the public has a distorted, simplistic image of the legislative process. But they accept that as a given, and for the most part they are comfortable with being held accountable on the basis of the visible, public part of what they do: speak, debate, testify, hold hearings, have press conferences, and vote. In this sense, legislators organize the arena and set the agenda for coverage, and the press accepts the terms.

Press acquiescence in this arrangement stems in part from the difficulty of getting at the behind-the-scenes side of the legislative process, in part from a lack of resources and the pressure of time, and in part from a need not to offend the individuals who provide them with access. It is complicated for a reporter to sort out a relationship with a congressman when the reporter is supposed to be holding the congressman accountable and the congressman is a crucial source of information as well.

Perhaps it is this last element that produces one of the aspects of congressional coverage most criticized by congressmen themselves. Those who work in Congress, members and staff, sense a strong streak of cynicism on the part of the press about the legislative process. Sometimes this is manifested in an apparent hostility to legislative politics, to the inevitable bargaining, compromising, and maneuvering politics entails. Legislators feel that many journalists highlight the negative aspects of legislative politics but fail to appreciate its positive functions in building consensus and in producing workable legislation.

Moreover, many legislators believe that even when the press has good reason to be critical of the legislative process, its diagnosis of the problem is superficial. In our interviews Congressman Barney Frank raised this issue when he argued that the press emphasizes the symptoms of systemic problems rather than their underlying causes. For example, the role and influence of lobbyists are often disparaged in the press, but coverage rarely shows how that influence really operates. Coverage also neglects the positive functions of lobbying in providing important information and in representing various social interests. Lou Cannon of the *Washington Post* agreed. In his view, the press is not doing the job it should in covering the connection between lobbying, campaign contributions, and legislative behavior. When they convey the impression that lobbyists or Political Action Committees simply buy congressional votes, the reporters are, in his words, "feeding on public skepticism" and vastly oversimplifying an exceedingly complex issue.

In a similar vein, Senator Paul Simon bemoaned the media's emphasis on attention-getting, yet trivial, issues rather than on substantive problems. As an example, Simon noted that foreign trips by members of Congress are ridiculed in the press, pejoratively called junkets, and treated as a waste of taxpayers' money. The reality, he argued, is that legislators do not travel abroad enough; they often lack firsthand knowledge of international problems and hence are at a disadvantage when they must deliberate on substantive foreign policy questions. All too often the press exposes junketing, which is an occasional, but not a systemic, abuse, but ignores legislative provincialism, which is a far deeper problem.

For their part, the journalists we interviewed explained part of the problem as a result of lack of resources. Reporters covering the Hill are expected to cover breaking news, and there is enough of that to keep them busy. In recent years some journalists, such as David Rogers, formerly of the *Boston Globe* and now of the *Wall Street Journal*, and Martin Tolchin of the *New York Times*, have been given the freedom by their news organizations to provide detailed reporting on the behind-the-scenes process in the Congress. Reporting of this kind is respected by legislators and journalists alike. It indicates what can be done if news organizations are willing to devote the time and resources that are required.

The strongest disagreement we discovered between journalists and legislators was over the impact that media coverage has on the legitimacy and effectiveness of Congress as an institution. Legislators argued that the way the Congress is covered unfairly demeans and undermines Congress as an institution and erodes public confidence in the legislative process. Reporters had distinctly different views. Either, as Judy Woodruff said, the press does not understand that their reportage shapes long-run public perceptions of the Congress as an institution, or, as Irwin Arieff implied, reporters simply do not believe that it is part of their responsibility to worry about such consequences. Either way, the issue is joined, and it is one that is central to the tension that does exist between the Congress and the press.

Conflicting Roles

Who represents the people? Ask a congressman and you will hear a ringing articulation of his or her duty to speak for the people back home. Ask a congressional reporter and you will hear the same duty cited, the duty to be the eyes and ears of the people who can't be in Washington to keep watch on the government themselves. Both legislators and journalists thus understand that they perform a representational function, yet they have clearly separate jobs and very different ways of going about their business. Much of the tension between the Congress and the media grows out of the gap between their shared sense of responsibility to reader/viewers and constituents and their very different organizational priorities, purposes, and needs.

Congress is designed to be open and accessible to a wide variety of influences, to address a broad range of issues, and to be very slow in making decisions. This is because one of its chief functions is to develop a broad social consensus. Lines of authority and decisionmaking in Congress are difficult to follow and understand. Congress is relatively nonhierarchical and flexible in its internal relations; the informal norms of comity, deference, and mutual respect are important ingredients in the process of legislative compromise and coalition building. Disagreements can be intense, but personal relationships are usually not allowed to become bitter.

These and similar institutional characteristics make it easier for Congress to perform its functions, but more difficult for news organizations to perform theirs. Newsmen need copy—right now, today, all the time. The staffing and assignment patterns of most news organizations are set up to accommodate mainly stories that can be covered in a few days at most. They are strained by the task of covering drawn-out and intermittent congressional proceedings. Reporters prefer drama and conflict, and in order to simplify their monitoring of information networks, they benefit from a clear sense of patterns of authority or authoritative comment in the institutions they cover. Congress occasionally provides the former, but very rarely the latter. White House correspondents, by contrast, know exactly where to go to at least try to find out what they want to know. Their problem is that information there is too well managed, too structured. Capitol Hill reporters are awash with information that is scarcely managed or centralized at all. There is not one Congress to cover, but 535 Congresses.

The Plural Media

Part of the complexity of the congressional-press relationship stems from the number and range of news organizations covering the Hill. Each news organization has its own individual culture and personality. Beyond that, different kinds of news organizations have different functions and play different roles in covering the Congress. There are several categories of news organizations that must be distinguished.

Television operates under very different pressures from those experienced by print journalists. Time constraints severely limit television's coverage of congressional life. Needing pictures to tell the story, the networks are often pushed toward personalizing issues, playing one member off against the other, as a way of covering the story. Those opportunities for documentaries with more in-depth coverage—"60 Minutes" and "20/20"—are by their nature geared toward the dramatic and sensational, rather than the typical and routine."Nightline"and "MacNeil-Lehrer News Hour" have more opportunity to present congressional practice in detail and issues in depth, and have often done so. With C-Span now providing extensive coverage of congressional proceedings, the networks have the opportunity to use excerpts of debates and hearings in their reports without having to film the entire proceedings themselves. On the other hand, the availability of this tape on a daily basis to the networks has given congressmen the opportunity to exploit the medium for their own purposes.

Turning to print journalism, there is a fundamental distinction between the state, regional, and local press on the one hand, and the national press on the other. As legislators themselves observed in our interviews, the relationship between a legislator and the state and local press tends to be very cozy. These are "soft presses";

they are not critical, and tend to rely on the legislator for their stories. The national press is, by contrast, much more critical and independent. Members of the national press corps in Washington typically do not have much direct personal contact with individual congressmen, especially House members. They are more oriented toward the congressional leadership and toward issues affecting Congress as a whole.[10]

The kind of access reporters from different kinds of news organizations need for the stories they are assigned to write is a crucial factor in shaping the dynamics of the journalist-legislator relationship. Reporters who cover Congress from regional or local newspapers are under tremendous and conflicting pressures to be the local congressman's critic on the one hand, and to get all his or her inside information on the other. One regional congressional correspondent with whom we spoke described in detail the difficulty of being a good reporter and thereby risking the possibility that her chief source—the local congressman—would deny her access. We found that these regional correspondents are stretched thin in their assignments, rarely have the time or resources to do extensive background research on stories they file, and suffer under the twin pressures described above. It is not surprising that their coverage tends to be supportive of the local congressman, and that the local congressman can often successfully initiate the coverage. Yet these newspapers provide a large portion of the independent information that constituents read about their legislator.

What we have referred to as the national press includes the *New York Times*, the *Washington Post*, the *Wall Street Journal*, the weekly news magazines, the three major networks, AP, UPI, National Public Radio, and the *Los Angeles Times*. All are important because they disseminate news about the Congress to the country at large. The *Post* and the *New York Times*, however, not only are important because they shape public opinion nationally and tell the congressmen what the folks back home are reading, but also because they serve a very special function as in-house governmental news organs. They play a significant role within Congress itself, because members of Congress often rely on these newspapers to learn what is going on in the rest of government, and even in the Congress itself. Each of these national news organizations has the financial and human resources that local and regional news organizations lack. It is understandable, therefore, that the national news organizations initiate most of the investigative stories involving the Congress, are the first to break stories involving political corruption and ethical abuse, and tend to provide more institutional coverage than other news organizations.

The Legislative Ethics Beat

When we asked reporters and legislators about the coverage of ethics, the responses made it clear that we had entered sensitive territory. In addition to the various problems and dilemmas discussed in Section I, we found that the legislative ethics beat is a locus of special pressures on the legislator-journalist relationship.

On the press side, the norm of objectivity makes journalists reluctant to cover ethical issues until they become so tangible that they are part of the public record. Journalists are reluctant to raise ethical issues or to analyze them on their own. For the most part they approach ethical issues only indirectly, through quotes elicited from others. As a result, legislative ethics is molded by journalistic practice into the form of charges and countercharges, accusations and denials. This distorts the process of moral dialogue and reflection in the legislative setting and leads to a preoccupation with what former Congressman Richardson Preyer called "scandal ethics."

Here again the pressure on journalists to maintain cordial working relationships with legislators they cover is important. It creates a major disincentive to report on unethical conduct until official charges have been brought. (Milton Hoffman of the Gannett chain, who has spent many years covering the New York State Assembly in Albany, suggested that the problem is even more acute at the state level where "extraordinary clubbishness" undermines the healthy arms-length relationship between journalists and legislators.)

James Wieghart, a longtime Washington journalist who now covers politics for the Scripps-Howard newspapers, suggested an additional reason why covering ethics is such a tricky business. Reporters, he noted, internalize the core values of journalism and of news organizations and then tend to assess the people and institutions they cover in terms of these values. When journalistic and legislative values conflict, or when the same values are interpreted differently by journalists and legislators, it is difficult for journalists to sort these conflicts out and to find the perspective needed to cover legislative ethics in a balanced fashion. Most reporters do not want to impose their own personal or professional values on legislators, nor do they want to be unduly deferential to the legislator's point of view.

To see this problem more clearly, consider the moral virtue of candor, a rather frequent bone of contention between the journalists and legislators we talked to. Candor is a cardinal virtue for journalists; they value it in themselves, and they respect it in their colleagues, their sources, and the legislators they cover. Thus, they are quick to condemn legislators who lack candor and who manipulate information in ways that journalists take to be self-serving. For legislators, candor occupies a different place in the scale of moral values. Legislators certainly respect candor, but they do not give it the same moral priority that journalists do, and they do not interpret the ethics of manipulating information in the same way. In legislative life information is a form of power, a resource to be used instrumentally to achieve other ends. When we asked journalists to describe their image of the "good legislator," candor figured prominently in their answers. When we asked legislators the same question, candor appeared as a much more qualified virtue; it could be a constructive or a destructive trait, depending on the circumstances.

This finding helps to explain why ethical issues are an especially problematical area of legislative life for journalists to cover. Whose standards, journalists rightfully ask, should they apply in covering legislative ethics? It also indicates the fact that the value systems growing out of journalistic and legislative practice do not overlap completely. The tension between these value systems is a function of many factors—the complex relationships between legislators and journalists, the differing institutional pressures and incentives affecting them, and the evolution of professional norms in journalism.

To reject, as we have, the notion that the relationship between journalists and legislators is or should be adversarial is not to disregard these important tensions and differences in their respective roles and values. Once these tensions have been acknowledged and put in their proper perspective, however, it is important not to lose sight of the equally important moral bonds that connect the work journalists should do with the work legislators should do in a democracy.

In the remainder of this essay we shall explore the ethical connection between journalists and legislators by analyzing the ethics of representation. Section III provides an account of the basic principles of legislative ethics, principles derived from the role legislators play in the representative system. These principles set the public standards journalists can and should use in covering congressional ethics and in interpreting and explaining the moral significance of legislative conduct. Section IV provides a parallel account of the basic principles of journalistic ethics, principles derived from the role congressional journalists play in the representative system. These principles offer public and professional standards that journalists should use in assessing their own conduct and the performance of news organizations.

III. The Ethics of Legislators as Elected Representatives

In the American political system, as in all other modern democracies, the fundamental role of the legislator is to represent the citizens—to bring their voice, their interests, their values and aspirations into the making of law and public policy. The theory and practice of representation provide the obvious starting point for an analysis of legislative ethics in a democracy.[11]

Principles of Legislative Ethics

In most writings on the subject, debate over the ethics of representation has centered on two competing conceptions: the "trustee" theory and the "delegate" theory. According to the trustee theory, election constitutes a broad transfer of authority from the represented to the representatives. In this view, the representative has a mandate to make legislative decisions based upon his or her own judgment of the best interests of the represented and the common good of the political community as a whole. What the representative (as trustee) owes constituents is simply his or her best effort to shape public policy wisely and intelligently.

The delegate theory, by contrast, emphasizes a considerably more constrained and specific relationship between the representative and the represented. According to this theory, representation involves the carrying out of a set of express or tacit instructions. Election constitutes a specific transfer of authority, and the representative has a moral duty to make legislative decisions in accordance with the expressed interests and preferences of the represented. What the representative as delegate owes constituents is strict adherence to their known preferences, and their continued support in subsequent elections is due primarily to his or her successful ability to deliver the benefits and protections they desire.

Neither of these theories provides a satisfactory account of the actual practice of representation, and neither provides a normative conception upon which the full range of a representative's ethical obligations could be grounded. Precisely because they are each simplified or abstract models of representation, they sidestep most of the hard questions of legislative ethics. These questions arise precisely because legislators are and must be both trustees and delegates: autonomous leaders who exercise their own independent judgment, and accountable servants of the people who give voice to and protect their constituents' interests. Neither an ethic of trusteeship nor an ethic of delegation fully captures the complex ethics of legislative life.

Moreover, legislators must be responsible members of legislative institutions. As individuals who represent others, they have an ethical obligation to contribute to a collective, institutionalized legislative process that makes effective representation possible. Political theorists Amy Gutmann and Dennis Thompson have made some pertinent comments on this issue:

> . . . Representation is not simply a one-to-one relation between constituents and legislators but a collective process involving systematic interaction among many people holding many different roles. It is this pattern of conduct in the representative system as a whole that should ultimately determine our moral and political judgments about legislative ethics . . . because legislators must choose among many different roles, and because the rightness of that choice depends on the state of the system in which they make it, legislative ethics cannot specify in advance a particular set of duties for a representative. Legislative ethics cannot tell the representative whether to act as a trustee or delegate even on a given issue, and certainly cannot tell him what position to take on the issue. It follows that legislative ethics will grant considerable discretion to legislators in their choices of roles in their decisions on policy.[12]

These considerations suggest that there are at least three fundamental ethical principles that should guide the legislator in conscientious discharge of his or her duties. These are the principles of autonomy, accountability, and responsibility.

Autonomy

The principle of legislative autonomy holds that legislators have an obligation to deliberate and decide free from improper influence. In legislative life it is impossible to ensure that all the decisions legislators make will be wise ones. But by taking steps to preserve the autonomy of their judgments, they can at least increase the probability that they will judge and decide correctly.

This is not to say that legislators should try to make decisions in some kind of vacuum. Isolating legislators from all outside influences would be both unworkable, unwise, and unacceptable from a democratic point of view. Democratic representation clearly requires that legislators remain open to many kinds of external influences, and that they be accessible and responsible to constituent interest and to the public interest. The problem, of course, is to draw the line between influences that are a normal part of a healthy democratic process and those that are improper. Improper influences are ones that tend to distract legislators from their basic democratic responsibilities. They draw the legislators' use of the authority and resources of their office away from the public ends—the representation of constituent interest and the promotion of the public interest—that these offices were created to serve in the first place.

The principle of autonomy reminds us that although legislators must take stands and have strong opinions, they must simultaneously continue to be open-minded and not beholden to any single group or to any special interest in reaching their decisions. They must always be attentive to the fullest possible range of various considerations that bear on the issues before them. In order to preserve their autonomy, legislators must avoid becoming too dependent upon any single source of information or analysis. Legislators who, in the overall pattern of the roles they play, become simply the spokesmen for the narrow interests and limited objectives of specially favored groups violate the principle of autonomy every bit as seriously as those who dispense legislative favors in return for financial benefits.

Accountability

The principle of legislative accountability holds that a legislator has an obligation to provide constituents with the information and understanding they require in order for them to exercise responsible democratic citizenship. Precisely because legislators have wide discretion in their activities, and because no theory of representation or legislative ethics can prescribe all the choices they must make, the ultimate check against improper legislative conduct and the ultimate support for proper legislative conduct must come from the voters themselves. This is the core of the traditional democratic idea that the authority of those who govern rests on the consent of those who are governed. The idea behind the principle of accountability is that legislators ought to take reasonable steps to ensure that that consent is fully informed and enlightened.

The principle of accountability is the basis for the various "public disclosure" measures enacted in recent years—financial disclosure, open meeting rules, disclosure of campaign contributions, and the like. These measures were designed to enable constituents to judge more effectively whether legislators are fulfilling their duty to preserve their autonomy. The moral justification for these laws and for the duty of legislators to comply with them comes from their obligation to be accountable.

Financial disclosure requirements have provided some information about legislators' personal and family economic ties and business associations. Yet it is clear that constituents need more than just financial information about those aspects of a legislator's personal associations that bear on the performance of his or her official duties. Full accountability requires not only that legislators should disclose what they have done, but also that they should explain what they have done. Too often, disclosure alone does not provide an effective deterrent to unethical conduct, because legislators realize that, even if certain information does become known, its significance will not be understood and its implications will not be perceived. Legislators must ask themselves whether constituents can understand the meaning of their actions and disclosures.

Responsibility

The principle of legislative responsibility holds that legislators have an obligation to contribute to the effective institutional functioning of the legislative process. Representation and lawmaking are collective processes; they rely on the cooperation and coordinated activities of many legislators. Therefore, individual legislators cannot fulfill the ethical obligations of their office or role merely by attending to their own activities and to their own relationship with their constituents. They must be concerned as well with the activities of other legislators, and with the representational functioning of the legislature as an institution.

Individual legislators may err in their judgment on policy issues and support ill-conceived measures. But the legislative system as a whole has evolved to compensate for those individual limitations. Hence, there is a paradoxical quality inherent in the relationship between individual legislators and the legislative process. In large measure, the legislative process is designed to compensate for, and to mitigate the harmful consequences of, the intellectual, political, and even moral mistakes that individual legislators inevitably make. But like all structural checks against human fallibility, in the final analysis legislative procedures cannot achieve these goals without the active support and cooperation of individual legislators themselves.

The principle of responsibility adds an important element to our analysis of legislative ethics, for it explains one of the features of the ethical duties of legislators that sets them apart from, and makes them more stringent than, the ordinary ethical duties of private citizens. In order to maintain public confidence in the institution and in the legislative process, lawmakers have a duty, not only to avoid wrongdoing, but also to avoid the appearance of wrongdoing.

It is a commonplace of political prudence that legislators must be concerned with their public image as well as their public performance, the appearance as well as the substance of what they do. The current Senate and House codes of ethics transform this prudential maxim into an ethical obligation by requiring not only that legislators avoid wrongdoing, but also that they avoid its appearance. Many have questioned the appropriateness of this so-called higher standard. Is it fair to expose legislators to moral censure (and sometimes to official censure) even though they have not committed any substantive wrong?

The principle of responsibility provides a rationale for this higher standard. The integrity of individual legislators and that of the legislature as a whole are inseparable. Individual legislators cannot effectively represent the interests of their constituents or promote the public interest on their own. They require the support of the legislative process as a whole to accomplish those ends. Similarly, malfeasance, or the public perception of malfeasance, not only discredits the guilty individual, it discredits the legislature as an institution and other legislators as a group as well. By performing the obligations of their office badly, individual legislators can make it much more difficult for other legislators to perform theirs well. Therefore legislatures are justified in condemning the behavior of individual legislators that casts the entire assembly into "dishonor and disrepute."

Legislative ethics pertains not only to the moral integrity of individual legislators, but to the moral climate within legislatures as well. How can Congress as an institution create within itself an organizational ethos and institutional arrangements that will support members in their efforts to fulfill their ethical duties? In our discussion of the principle of responsibility, we argued that legislators have an obligation to support and improve the functioning of the legislative process as a whole, in line with basic democratic values. Now we shall turn the question around and focus on what might be called the "moral ecology" of Congress.

Discussions of legislative ethics sometimes suggest that ethical reflection and decisionmaking are essentially individualistic activities that take place in the privacy of legislators' own consciences. Yet there is also an important collective or social dimension to ethical decisionmaking. Legislators, as moral agents, do have to make their own judgments, to be sure. But legislators need not—and should not—live out their moral lives in lonely isolation. Ethical choices should not be made in a social vacuum; they can be embedded in the ethos of a community of peers and woven through a rich fabric of collegial ties. The character of their social and institutional relationships has a substantial effect on the ability of legislators to understand and fulfill their ethical duties.

In recent years there has been an erosion of traditional, informal norms and a trend toward an increasing atomization within Congress. Legislators receive less institutional guidance than they once did; they are increasingly—but of course not totally—on their own, institutionally, politically, and ethically. A burdensome legislative workload and the growing layers of staff that mediate between legislators and their colleagues make it more difficult for legislators to work closely with one another or to form close personal ties. These developments point to problems inasmuch as they have swept away many of the older, informal systems of ethical norms that Congress once provided for its members. But these changes present new opportunities and creative possibilities as well. Few would want to return to the dictatorial leadership, powerful ruling cliques, and committee fiefdoms that once dominated Congress. As the vacuum left by the passing of older customs and conventions is filled by newly created systems of ethical support, Congress has an important opportunity to provide its members with institutional incentives and guidance based on a new and better understanding of legislative ethics.

The Media's Role

One can hardly overemphasize the significance of the media's role in enhancing legislative ethics in all of its various dimensions. Journalists can and should publicly evaluate individual legislators and Congress as a whole in accordance with the principles we have outlined. For if the press does not evaluate legislators by these ethical standards, it is unlikely that the citizenry will be willing or able to do so either.

Moreover, journalists must not only evaluate and judge ethically, they must also assist legislators in fulfilling these ethical obligations. The press can enhance autonomy by helping to provide the information legislators need to remain fully and adequately informed on policy issues. Journalists should expose cases of undue influence where they exist and, equally important, should not neglect positive coverage of cases where legislative autonomy is exercised.

In order to enhance accountability, journalists should strive to ensure that their coverage of legislative activity does in fact contribute to the enhancement of their readers' and viewers' capacity to exercise their rights as citizens. Journalists should expand their coverage of legislative ethics issues to convey the complexity of ethical dilemmas in legislative life. Media coverage focusing exclusively on scandals or extreme cases of unethical conduct is not sufficient. Ethical decisionmaking is an ongoing reality in Congress; it should also be an ongoing story for the press.

Finally, journalists can enhance legislative responsibility by promoting better public understanding of the institutional functioning of legislatures. They should nurture public tolerance of the healthy checks and balances of the legislative process, but they should also help to create public support for legislative modernization and reform. The media affects the pressures and incentives at work within Congress to a greater degree than most journalists seem to recognize. Earlier we commented on some of the unintentional ways in which this influence has impeded the successful functioning of ethical reforms, such as financial disclosure and the work of the House and Senate ethics committees. But there is no reason, in principle, why this need be the case. The media have the capacity, the resources, and the skills that would permit them to reinforce the efforts of conscientious legislators to maintain a positive ethical climate and ethos in Congress. The ethical obligations of journalists as actors in the system of democratic representation suggests that the media should use their resources to this end. Whether they will do so is a question that only journalists themselves can answer.

IV. The Ethics of Journalists as Unelected Representatives

To many journalists, any systematic attempt to prescribe ethical principles for the practice of the profession of journalism is an inherently misguided, even dangerous, enterprise. They do not hold this view out of a failure to appreciate the importance of ethics or because they do not face ethical issues in their work. Indeed, as a recent study by Citizen's Choice, Inc., *Responsibility and Freedom in the Press*, observed: "The journalist who has not struggled with himself or herself and with colleagues on questions of ethics and the role of the press is increasingly rare today."[13] Rather, the nervousness that journalists often feel when presented with theories of journalism ethics comes from the specter of ethics codes, regulations, and restraints imposed upon them from the outside. Too much public concern with journalism ethics, they feel, is a sign that their freedom—press freedom—is under seige.

Partly for these reasons, perhaps, the press side of the ethical connection between Congress and the media—that is, those special ethical obligations incumbent on journalists in covering legislators and the legislative process—has not received sufficient attention or analysis in the past. When it comes to reporting on the lives of private citizens, business activities, court proceedings, and the like, journalists readily acknowledge that they must struggle to balance freedom of the press with potentially conflicting values, such as privacy, legal due process, and the protection of vulnerable individuals whose lives and standing in the community can be drastically affected by publicity. In these areas the press often quietly exercises self-restraint, and tacit notions of journalism ethics are built into judgments of newsworthiness, balance, and fairness. But when powerful government institutions and officials are the subjects of news coverage and analysis, the values to be balanced against aggressive reporting are not so clear, and the case for journalistic self-restraint in the name of ethical responsibility seems much harder to make.

We believe that this case indeed is—and should be—hard to make. But we also believe that it reasonably can be—and, again, should be—made sometimes. The essence of the case for ethical constraints in media coverage of Congress comes not so much from moral obligations journalists owe individual legislators, or Congress as an institution, as from their obligations to the process of legislative representation, a process of which journalists themselves are a part. These obligations will be more clearly perceived and understood if we recognize two key points. First, that the congressional journalist is a special kind of unelected representative; and, second, that the role journalists play and the freedom with which they are entrusted are legitimate and proper only to the extent that the representational functions they perform constructively complement and supplement those of legislators. Here, drawing on our preceding analysis of the principles of legislative ethics, we offer parallel principles of journalism ethics designed to clarify the nature and democratic rationale of the obligations owed to the process of legislative representation. These principles and obligations define the press's side of the ethical connection between Congress and the media.

Before turning to these principles and obligations, we must first briefly consider the question of journalism ethics in general. At the present time there is little, if any, clear consensus about the philosophical foundations of journalism ethics that could guide the discussion of the ethical dimensions of media coverage of Congress. Ultimately, perhaps, a better understanding of the ethics of congressional journalism may shed some new light on the general ethical foundations of professional journalism and its place in society at large.

The Foundations of Journalism Ethics

All discussions of ethical foundations in journalism are colored by the great social value that has been placed on a free press by our constitutional, democratic tradition. This tradition has led many journalists to resist the very idea of any generally applicable ethical standards. In their view, it is up to each journalist to develop his or her own individual moral code. The so-called absolutist view of the First Amendment holds that the social value of a free press must prevail over other social values and interests. It also holds that any efforts to establish ethical codes or rules run counter to the spirit, if not the letter, of the First Amendment. This is not a sophisticated legal or ethical argument. It is an attitude and a sentiment that is rooted deeply in the moral sensibility of American journalism today. It is also an attitude fraught with great risks.

First, if journalists tell society that this interpretation of the First Amendment is the essence of journalism ethics, then they turn all ethical issues into legal issues and make the Supreme Court the final arbiter in both spheres. Even more worrisome, such a position provides those in our society who do not give the value of a free press overriding priority with an open invitation to push for statutory and even constitutional restrictions. The Court has already demonstrated over and over again that it is willing to limit press freedom (the regulation of broadcasting and the libel laws are two examples); inviting new confrontations is not the way to secure broad social support for a free press. Moreover, it is dangerous to blur the distinction between legal and ethical considerations. What a journalist may do legally is different from what a journalist ought to do. Simply because a court decides not to put a reporter in jail, slap an editor with a fine, or otherwise penalize some action by a news organization does not automatically mean that the action is morally justified. If that were the case, then the lowest form of legally permissible behavior would have to be understood as morally correct; few would be willing to go that far.

There is no widely accepted philosophical foundation for the ethics of the American press, even though there have been serious attempts to develop one. In two seminal works, *Public Opinion* and *The Phantom Public*, Walter Lippmann articulated a theory of the role of the press in public affairs that had significant philosophical and ethical implications. His books reflected his own increasing disenchantment with the classic view of democracy as an interested and aware citizenry taking an active part in policymaking. Lippmann quite rightly understood what most Americans now take for granted, namely that elites and special interests are more involved in public affairs than other people, and that the press cannot and should not try to pursue the phantom of a fully informed electorate. The press, he said, is in the fact business, not the truth business, and the best it can do is present the facts so that a few people with sufficient discernment and expertise can sort the information out and make some truth of it. He also believed that there was no possibility that the general public could be informed enough to participate actively across a range of policy areas. The best the press could do, he thought, was to provide for the public a kind of general framework for what was happening so that at election time, and occasionally on issues of overriding importance, an intelligent, if not fully informed, public could play a role.

As Michael Schudson has pointed out, Lippmann's pessimistic view seems to have taken hold more with political scientists than with journalists. Political scientists have studied the role of mediating institutions, such as the press and interest groups, with a vengeance, while journalists by and large cling to the notion that they are making pure democracy work, without accepting the limitations either on their capacity and or on that of the citizenry for pulling it off.

In retrospect, then, Lippmann's work achieved two things that contemporary discussions of journalism ethics cannot afford to ignore. First, he focused attention on the role of the press in public affairs. It is no longer credible to argue that the practice of journalism does not affect the democratic process, or that journalists ought not, in principle, be concerned with their impact on that process. Second, he called attention to the fact that in its role in public affairs, the press has a different function with respect to elites than it does with respect to other citizens. The press plays a special role in providing communication among those who exercise particular influence in the governing process; it is critically important and not at all similar to the function it fills with respect to the public at large. The notion of multiple press roles and responsibilities is an important contribution to understanding the ethical dimensions of the relationship between the press and the legislative process.

The next landmark in press ethics after Lippmann is the report of the Hutchins Commission issued in 1948.[14] The Commission developed what is now called the social responsibility theory of the press. According to this theory, the press has a responsibility to the community it serves; that responsibility manifests itself in the standards of performance and the determination of what is news. The central notion was that freedom of the press, as guaranteed in the First Amendment and supported in principle as a shared value in the country, carries with it some concomitant obligations. When the Hutchins Commission's report first appeared, it met with an extremely cool reception in the journalism community. But since that time the idea of social responsibility has spread in journalism, as it has in many other professions. It has been reflected in journalism school curricula and in the institutionalization of the ombudsman role on many newspapers. If the social responsibility theory has not provided secure philosophical foundation for journalism ethics, at least it has pointed out, as Lippmann did in his own way, the linkage between the social and political power inherent in the influence journalists exercise and their ethical obligations.

Principles of Journalism Ethics

How do congressional journalists think about their ethical obligations in covering Congress?

Some journalists—a tiny minority, we believe—think about them not at all, as a matter of principle. They see themselves as operating under a kind of John Wayne school of press philosophy: no rules of the road, every man for himself, it's kill or be killed. They see their responsibilities, if at all, as being only to the company that pays their salaries.

Far more prevalent is the view in which journalists see themselves as providing the information necessary for citizens to make informed decisions, and they take this responsibility seriously. In the extreme view, this notion rests on a theory of pure democracy, which suggests that the people play an ongoing role in the decisionmakng process. In a more modest view, such as the one proposed by Lippmann, the press plays a role in providing citizens with what they need to know to vote at election time with intelligence, if not with complete information, and perhaps in between elections to provide people with a broad outline of policy direction so that they have a sense of where things are going.

Then there are those reporters who see themselves as the watchdogs for the people, holding public officials' feet to the fire, rooting out corruption, picking up the responsibility that busy citizens cannot shoulder.

There are also those who see themselves as the adversary of government, committed to being the opposition, no matter who is in power and what they are doing.

Finally, there are elements of the press, such as the wire services, who see themselves as transmitters, reporters of record, whose job it is to broadcast or send out everything that happens and let the various news organizations or other clients decide what to pass along any further.

We could go on and on, listing various views of press responsibility that derive either from some theoretical notion of what the role of the press ought to be or from some anecdotal or systematic idea about what it actually is. What is important to note is that these views have to do in one way or another with the fact that journalists function as surrogates or stand-ins for their readers or listeners; they get the information citizens cannot get for themselves, they watch out for citizens' interests, and keep legislators accountable. In a word, journalists function as "representatives" in a special but significant and important sense of that term.

To ask about the obligations of journalists who cover Congress, then, is to ask about their ethical obligations as representatives, or at least quasi-representatives, in the democratic system. As we have suggested, journalists represent absent citizens in the legislative process by providing them (in theory at least) with the information and understanding they would acquire if they were present in Washington themselves. Equally important, journalists affect the ability of congressmen—the formal, elected representatives—to carry out their representational duties.

For their part, legislators are quick to acknowledge this. They know that they need the press if they are to perform their representative function. Legislatures need the press if they are to satisfy their constitutional responsibilities. Readers and viewers need the press if they are to perform their duties as citizens in a democracy. Various readers and viewers need the press for different reasons; that is, people with special interests in legislation need to know a lot more and need it on a more timely basis than do those who have only a general interest.

The way the press does its job, the standards it follows, and the mission it pursues will affect the activity of legislators, the performance of legislatures, and the understanding of citizens. In addition, the way individual reporters do their jobs will affect the public credibility of other journalists and of news organizations.

The insight that reporters and news organizations form a crucial link in the representative process holds at least two important implications for the press. First, since journalists are in some respects representatives of their constituents (their readers and viewers), they have duties to their constituents that derive directly from their representative role. In this regard, the ethical obligations of journalists and those of legislators overlap to a much greater degree than is often recognized.

In addition, journalists have duties to the representational system of which they are a part. They have duties both to the part of the representational system that involves them directly, namely the flow of information between legislators and constituents, and to the part of the system they influence only from the outside, namely the legislative and electoral process.

In Section III we introduced three ethical principles—autonomy, accountability, and responsibility—that constitute the basis of representational obligations in general, and we applied these principles to legislators, the elected representatives of our democratic system. Here we propose to apply these principles to the analogous situation of congressional journalists.

Autonomy

The principle of journalistic autonomy holds that journalists should make reporting and editorial decisions free from improper influences. Journalists must strive to remain open-minded, adequately and independently informed, and must avoid placing themselves or being placed in situations that would compromise their independent judgment through coercion, bias, or conflict of interest. The principle of autonomy is closely related to the traditional journalistic norm of objectivity, but it suggests a much less passive and reactive image of the journalist as an ethical actor and decisionmaker. In this way, the notion of autonomy incorporates and acknowledges the kernel of truth contained in recent critiques of traditional conceptions of objectivity. Journalists are not simply neutral conduits of information or facts. All reporting, let alone editing, analysis, and commentary, is an unavoidably active, selective, and interpretive process. This does not mean that there is no possible line to be drawn between journalism and literature or fiction, as Janet Cooke and others have discovered. But it does mean that journalistic decisionmaking involves all the characteristic ingredients of human judgment—discernment, selectivity, setting priorities, and balancing conflicting values—and as such is subject to a broad range of influences.

What then does it mean for a journalist to be free from improper influence? What constitutes improper influence? Here, as with legislators, financial conflicts of interest represent an obvious source of pressure that tends to compromise journalistic autonomy. Similarly, if a journalist would stand to gain politically (as a member of a political party) or professionally (by cutting corners in order to get a scoop), autonomy is undermined. Finally, autonomy can be compromised when a journalist stands to gain ideologically; that is, where his or her views about what is good public policy affect what is reported and how it is reported. If the journalist is committed to furthering a point of view, a particular point of view, then the journalist is not acting as an ethically autonomous representative unless he or she shares that perception or commitment with the readers, sharing, either in the sense of having it in common, or in the sense of disclosure.

Autonomy requires open-mindedness, listening carefully to all sides and reflecting on them. In the course of their work, journalists necessarily form associations with people who have special interests and axes to grind. Autonomy means not being dependent on a single source of information and not allowing the value of a source of information to turn into an obligation to that source. It means separating professional and personal relationships, so that the interests of the latter do not undermine the responsibilities of the former. It means being willing to refuse honoraria, free trips, and perks on Capitol Hill. And it means remaining insulated from the business or economic interests of the corporate entity that owns the news organization.

Accountability

The principle of journalistic accountability holds that journalists have an obligation to use sources of information and the resources of news organizations to provide readers and viewers with the information and understanding they require in order to exercise responsible democratic citizenship. Just as legislators have an obligation to take reasonable steps to ensure that the democratic consent and mandate they receive from constituents is fully informed and enlightened, so journalists too have an obligation to promote the same end.

Here, surely, the ethical connection between journalists and legislators is most direct and telling. Legislators cannot fulfill their duty to be accountable without using the media as a vehicle of communicaton between themselves and their constituents. In this sense, the media provide a key element in making ethical legislative representation possible. At the same time, journalists also fulfill their obligation to be accountable, thereby creating a positive incentive for legislators to fulfill theirs. Without a press that looks out after the quality and quantity of political information available to the citizenry, it is likely that legislators would not be as open and as forthcoming as they are.

Saying this does not contradict what we said earlier about the ways media coverage tends to create defensiveness among legislators—a syndrome especially evident in the coverage of legislative ethics and closely related issues, such as congressional salaries, foreign travel, and the like. When that defensiveness in reaction to coverage is warranted (and it is not always), it is questionable whether the coverage is ethically justified according to the principle of accountability. If Senator Paul Simon, for example, is correct in saying that the press sensationalizes the relatively minor problem of junketing, but ignores or even exacerbates the much more serious problem of congressional provincialism in issues of foreign affairs, then that indicates the congressional journalists are not doing what the principle of accountability ethically requires.

Applying the principle of accountability to journalists as well as legislators reminds us of the fact that Congress and the press are both integral elements in a system of political communication and dialogue that makes contemporary democracy possible. When both sides fulfill their obligations under the principle of accountability, the representational process can function as it was intended to. When one side falls down on the job, the other can compensate for that failing. If both sides fail, our democracy is in jeopardy.

What makes a journalist accountable? One support for journalistic accountability can come from the news organization itself: substantial letters-to-the-editor space, accessible op-ed pages, and comprehensive corrections policies. Is the management willing to hear what critics, subjects of stories, consumers of stories, and outsiders have to say? As far as the news organization is concerned, are those explicit standards and principles for its reporters enforceable and enforced?

Next, there is the accountability of the reporter to the consumers of the news. Part of this involves disclosure: of financial interests, of entangling personal relationships, of an attitudinal bias one way or the other toward individual legislators or public policies. The other part comes from access: is the reporter available to talk with readers and viewers, to answer questions, to respond to criticisms? Is the news organization open about its decisionmaking and its standards for judgment? Is there an analogy for news organizations in the open meeting laws which news organizations, by and large, have helped to institute in legislatures?

The question is, what do consumers/constituents need to know in order to assess, evaluate, and use the information they are getting from the media? Legislator accountability is assured, in large part, by a vigilant press and by political opposition, both within the legislature and at home at election time. What is the corresponding pressure on reporters covering legislatures? Some accountability is assured by competitive news organizations where they exist, and some by the power of public officials to bypass the press and go straight to their shared constituents.

Although the legislator's constituents are the same as those of the journalist, these elements of accountability do not add up in either quality or quantity to what a legislator has to face. Nonetheless, like legislators, journalists should ask themselves, "Could I publicly justify doing this if my reader/viewers were fully informed about and fully understood what I have done?"

Responsibility

The principle of journalistic responsibility holds that journalists have an obligation to contribute to the effective institutional functioning of news organizations in order to make their role in the overall process of representation autonomous and accountable. Like individual legislators who serve in legislative institutions and must be responsible participants in a collective legislative process, individual journalists also have ethical obligations as members of news organizations and as participants in a process of reporting.

On one level, the principle of responsibility brings us back to the vexed problem of ethical self-regulation within the profession of journalism and within particular news organizations. The public credibility of all journalists is eroded by the unethical conduct of a few. As difficult as professional self-regulation is to achieve, within the constraints of prevailing attitudes among journalists and concerns about the weakening of First Amendment values, self-interest alone would suggest that it is not an issue contemporary journalism can afford to ignore. And the principle of responsibility suggests that more than mere self-interest is at stake.

Moreover, the principle of responsibility calls attention to the fact that any individual journalist's ability to perform his or her role ethically is at least partially dependent upon the conduct of other journalists and upon the ethical ethos or climate that is established within his or her newsroom. Conscientious journalists have an interest in helping to maintain an organizational ethos that supports autonomous and accountable journalistic decisionmaking; they also have an obligation to contribute to that ethos or to help create it when it does not exist. While the burden of this responsibility falls on all journalists, it is especially significant for senior correspondents, editors, and publishers who are in a position to influence policy and who serve as ethical role models within news organizations.

The principle of responsibility suggests finally that individual journalists should be attentive to the effects the policies and conduct of their news organizations are having on the public's understanding of the nature of the legislative process and of the strengths and weaknesses of Congress as an institution. This in a sense is the corollary of their duties defined by the principle of accountability.

In short, there is a triple responsibility for reporters covering legislatures: to the system of representative government of which they, like it or not, are a part; to their own news organizations; and to other journalists as members of the same craft or profession.

What is the responsibility of journalists to the system in which they work, namely, representative government? Michael Schudson provides one answer to this question when he argues that journalists need to act as though they lived in two different worlds: the world of the legislature and the system as it might be in some realm of ideal democracy, and the world of the legislature as it is in the real realm of imperfect democracy.[15] He wants the press to champion the kind of democracy that the textbooks write about, while also responding to the realities of legislative life and legislator-constituent relationships. Reporters must balance taking the legislature as it is, on its own terms, and trying to put it closer to the ideal. Don't pretend that the legislator or the legislature is something that it isn't, or can deliver something that it can't. Maybe, then, don't do the predictable prorogation story showing legislators sleeping on couches or, similarly, the ritual story about all the silly bills that are filed.

The significant point here is that journalists do have a special kind of responsibility for the proper functioning of the legislative/representative system. They have a relationship to the legislative system in the same way they have a responsibility to the news organizations they work for, to journalism itself, and to other reporters. Some of the implications of this analysis of journalistic responsibility are that journalists have an obligation to see to it that news organizations support coverage that: (1) looks for the workhorses who do the work rather than the showhorses who are there at the press conferences; (2) spotlights the points in the process where the real work is done, as in committees, rather than where the credit is distributed and the show is the thing, as in floor debates; and (3) pays attention and gives focus to the rules, procedures, and tactics that support or undermine the legislative process and individual legislators in their own efforts to be autonomous, accountable, and responsible.

Constraints

There are two kinds of constraints that hamper the ability of journalists to fulfill their duties of autonomy, accountability, and responsibility in covering Congress. The first involves competing pressures on their conduct from within journalism. The second has to do with impediments posed by Congress itself. Journalists and legislators who were consulted during this study identified a number of problems facing reporters that impede autonomous, accountable, and responsible conduct.

One constraint is the conventional definition of what constitutes news. News tends to be that which is unusual, dramatic, sensational, and personal. It emphasizes the individual over the institution, the conflict over the consensus, the mistakes over the good deeds, and the freak over the routine. News, especially news about legislatures, tends to be extremely episodic rather than continuous. The unfortunate implication of this is that it leads viewers and readers to think of legislatures as places characterized by individual posturing, petty conflict, gaffes, inefficiency, and, occasionally, an unusual scandal.

Various constraints are also imposed by the professional incentives in the journalism business. Career advancement in journalism is enhanced more by dramatic leaps than by slow, steady growth. This puts a tremendous premium on being on the front page (or high up in the newscast) and winning prizes. Stories that fall into those categories are characterized by being either very important, like the annual budget or a major vote on a major bill, or by being sensational and dramatic, ideally tinged with scandal or misfeasance. This provides an understandable, and in many respects, healthy inducement for journalists to do investigative work and develop their own stories, as well as to try to cover the big stories that are inevitably going to be prominently displayed. When the emphasis on the need for revelation results in disproportionate dominance of those stories—and the underrepresentation of more regular reporting of legislative business—this constraint begins to have important and discouraging consequences for public understanding of the functioning of the legislative process. Competition with other types of stories for scarce news space compounds this problem. News about legislatures is not on any front page editor's or news director's "must" list. In order to become a priority, legislative news must not only be more compelling than other news—and more compelling often means more dramatic—but more important to the public interest in the long run.

Another constraint comes from prevailing attitudes within the Washington press corps itself. Journalists develop—if they do not bring to their jobs—a healthy and necessary skepticism about the people and practices in high places. Honest skepticism, if pushed too hard, quickly turns into cynicism and results in stories about the legislative process and about individuals within it in which everyone's motives are doubted and the institution is assumed to be working against the public interest.

At the other extreme several journalists and legislators we interviewed were concerned about the pressure to develop a close personal relationship between reporters and legislators. As we mentioned earlier, this tends to be more of a problem for journalists from local or regional newspapers than for the national media. (It is also an especially difficult problem for reporters covering state legislatures.) But no congressional journalists are completely immune.

The second category of constraints are those imposed by the Congress as an institution. Candid journalists acknowledge that on the whole the Congress does not impose substantial institutional impediments to reporting. It is an extraordinarily accessible institution, consisting of a large number of people who know a lot of interesting information. Many members of Congress consider dealing with the press one of their major responsibilities. Still, there are constraints inherent in the institution that impede reporters from satisfying their highest ethical obligations.

To begin with, it is hard to know where the real work is done in the Congress. Because most legislators are conscious of their images and of the need for having good press, much of the work that is done in public is done primarily for press and public consumption. In some respects, the more the press probes behind the scenes, the further behind the scenes the real work will be done. This tension is demonstrated in part by the tacit distinction legislators make between their colleagues who work at the job and those who are only sure to be there when there is some credit to share. Inside the Congress, the members who do the dogged work of drafting legislation, working out compromises, and negotiating with interest groups are respected and appreciated. But one of the trade-offs they make in order to be effective is to let others steal the thunder. For the press this poses a problem: the ones who take credit for success are often not the ones who really deserve it.

Other aspects of Congress and the legislative process that make them difficult for journalists to cover include:

• *Time.* The process of building legislative consensus can be very slow; a bill may take months or years to work its way through the labyrinth.

• *Space.* While the legislature is in full swing, there may be literally dozens of newsworthy events going on at the same moment in different parts of the building: committee hearings, mark-up sessions, leaders' meetings, floor debate, bill signing, bill introduction, citizen protest, and the like.

• *Process.* In its simplest form, the process by which a bill becomes law is long and tortuous. Added to that are the conventions and mysteries that build up over time, and the rules themselves that are technical and intricate.

• *Motivations.* Even the most candid members often cannot

or will not describe the precise combination of motives that resulted in their taking a particular action or voting a particular way. Yet, sorting out why legislators did what they did may be as important to the reader/viewer as knowing what they did.

- *Substance.* Increasingly, Congress is being forced to deal with exceedingly complex policy issues, e.g., environmental risk assessments, budgetary and tax policy, and the like. This is a function of the recent reassertion of congressional power in the face of the so-called "Imperial Presidency." Reporting on such matters is doubly difficult; difficult to understand and difficult to explain to others.

- *Authority.* Where does authority lie in the legislature? Who has the power? Some power is formal, and therefore readily discernible, but much of the power of individuals in the legislative process comes from knowledge, personality, longevity, personal relationships, and similar factors that are harder to ascertain and difficult to reflect in reporting. Recent rules changes which have decentralized power in Congress have increased this problem for reporters.[16]

V. Journalism and the Ethics of Legislative Life

Legislative representation is a system encompassing many different actors and organizations linked together—sometimes cooperatively, sometimes competitively—by the representational functions they perform. Individual legislators and Congress as an institution bear the primary constitutional—and ethical—responsibility for providing citizens with democratic political representation. But the activities of legislators and the internal operations of Congress are but one focal point for a much broader representational process, an extremely important focal point, to be sure, but simply one focal point nonetheless.

Citizens are represented in various ways by executive branch officials and agencies; by organized lobbies, interest groups, trade unions, and professional associations; and, finally, in the sense we have been exploring in this essay, by journalists and news organizations. Without the support—and the restraints—provided by these outside representatives, neither individual legislators nor Congress as a whole would be able to provide effective, well-informed, accountable representation to their constituents. To gain a sense of unmet legislative needs and the interests to be balanced in their decisions, legislators can no longer rely exclusively, or even primarily, on direct communication with constituents or on their necessarily limited network of personal contacts in their districts. The relationships between legislators and their constituents are increasingly mediated by contacts with individuals and groups who purport to "represent" constituents in ways legislators cannot. Similarly, Congress cannot rely solely on its own internal resources—the information, knowledge, or expertise of members and staff—to perform its many legislative tasks. It too must draw upon the skills and services offered by outsiders, in order to provide effective representation to the nation as a whole in the demanding quest for laws and policies that serve the public interest.

In short, representation in a large, complex democratic society like the United States is a multifaceted, collective activity that flows through many layers. Needs and interests are presented and re-presented many times as they move upward in the political system from private citizens to congressmen. The quality of the official, de jure representation legislators provide citizens depends, in large measure, upon the kind of unofficial, de facto representation provided by individuals and groups at various levels of the representational system.

This perspective on the systemic nature of legislative representation has been the basis for our discussion of the ethical connection between Congress and the media. At least in their coverage of Congress and legislative affairs (and perhaps in other aspects of their work as well), journalists and news organizations are important actors in the representational system. Like legislators and all other actors in that system, they share the general representational obligations of autonomy, accountability, and responsibility. Legislative ethics is built around these basic obligations as they are applied to the specific characteristics of the legislator's function and role. That portion of professional journalism ethics pertaining to media coverage of Congress is built around these basic obligations as they are applied to the different functions and roles performed by journalists and news organizations.

Having discussed how legislators and journalists might exercise autonomy, accountability, and responsibility in their own respective niches in the representational system, it remains for us to tie together these parallel ethics and to show the connection between them. Neither journalists nor legislators can exercise their respective representational obligations in isolation from one another. The capacity of legislators to be autonomous, accountable, and responsible is affected by the way journalists perform their tasks. Conversely, the capacity of journalists to fulfill their representational obligations is affected by the conduct of legislators. No account of legislative ethics or this aspect of journalistic ethics would be complete without a consideration of this interconnection and mutual ethical interdependency. Drawing this connection brings us back to the specific example from which we started: media coverage of the ethics of legislative life.

Despite the fact that Congress has been going through a period of extensive ethics reform for the past decade, most people are not aware of the precise content of these reforms. Nor do they understand the events that led up to these reforms, the pressures and compromises that molded them, or, except perhaps in a vague and abstract way, the basic ethical rationales justifying those reforms and giving them substance.

If the general public is not very well informed about current ethical standards and regulations in Congress, unfortunately neither are congressmen themselves. With a few notable exceptions, members have generally not taken the time to study and reflect upon the ethical standards contained in the congressional ethics codes and in various statutes such as the Ethics in Government Act and the federal election laws. Ethics regulations, such as financial disclosure requirements, rules concerning the receipt of gifts and honoraria, and provisions designed to deter conflicts of interest, have become simply one more set of rules to follow, one more addition to the complex maze of procedural red tape in an institution already straining under the weight of formal procedures and paperwork. In the minds of many congressmen these ethics regulations are an irksome nuisance at best, a potentially dangerous political land mine at worst. The rules are complex and difficult to interpret; some members feel that they need a full-time staff person just to keep track of the various ethics provisions and to make sure that all the forms have been filled out properly.

Failure to comply with the regulations, whether willful or inadvertent, has devastating consequences. Congressmen have thus learned to live with the tighter, more exacting ethics regulations of the post-Watergate era with a mixture of resignation and wariness. They have learned to comply with ethical standards in much the same way as they cope with and dodge other potential sources of political risk, criticism, and damaging publicity.

No doubt this portrait is overdrawn. But it does capture one aspect of the attitude we have observed among congressmen and staff, an attitude engendered by the formalization of ethical standards in recent years. Perhaps such an attitude is unavoidable; it has also arisen among other professional groups that have resorted to legislative ethics codes and bureaucratic compliance mechanisms. However, when this legalistic mind-set prevails, the broader moral meaning and spirit of specific ethics provisions are lost. A focus on the strict compliance with ethical rules (institutionalized as legal rules and organizational policies) can easily eclipse more positive moral aspirations, ideals, and a sensitivity to the broader moral, civic, and humane purposes served by the representative's function and role.

At its best, media coverage of legislative ethics can serve to offset this legalistic mentality. It can place ethical rules in a broader historical and philosophical context. Stories about allegations of rule violations and investigative proceedings can be an occasion to remind legislators and citizens of the more general ethical ends these regulations are supposed to serve.

Unfortunately, it is equally easy—and probably much more

common—for media coverage to reinforce the legalistic attitude congressmen have toward their own ethical obligations. If legislators often view formal ethics regulations as so many bureaucratic snares, and look upon ethics committees, political opponents, and the press as so many predators waiting to pounce on those who run afoul of these formal rules, then journalists often contribute to this attitude by behaving in exactly this stereotypical fashion. It is not uncommon for reporters themselves to adopt this legalistic outlook on legislative ethics. Their stories are usually shaped precisely by the fact that a congressman has been caught in an ethical snare. That, to them, is the news. As the coverage unfolds in the ensuing days or weeks, the story focuses on how the congressman tries to wiggle free and on how others snipe and bite at the now vulnerable and exposed figure.

In all this—the nature of the snare itself, why it was put in place, and what it is supposed to do (other than to provide a periodic occasion for dramatic scandal and political conflict)—all these issues get lost, together with substantive questions about the moral ideals of representation and the public trust which may or may not have been violated by the congressman's conduct. In short, not *why* he or she ran afoul of the rules, but simply *that* he or she ran afoul of the rules becomes the only story that gets told.

This is not to say that the "that" story is an unfair, inappropriate, or nonnewsworthy story to run. Highlighting the political context and the political drama surrounding a legislative ethics story is clearly important and informative, as are the legal and institutional ramifications of particular ethics cases. The troubling aspect of the coverage of legislative ethics arises when the "that" story completely dominates the coverage—and hence public attention—and the "why" story gets buried and neglected in the process.

We believe that there is no intrinsic reason why the coverage of legislative ethics need be dominated by stories that, explicitly or implicitly, treat ethics regulations as moral snares. Journalists can reexamine and question their own legalistic attitude toward the rules, principles, and ideals of legislative ethics. This can help legislators reexamine their own legalistic orientation in the bargain. Journalists can readily go beyond the bureaucratic, procedural level of these events, and even go beyond the political angle, to sound out the moral meaning and the civic stakes involved in legislative ethics. This can and should be seen as a creative challenge for professional journalists. It is a challenge that will call upon journalists to develop a more complete philosophical and historical perspective on the moral meaning of legislative representation in a democratic society and to communicate these perspectives to their readers. It is a challenge that, thus far, has not been successfully met on the legislative ethics beat. Perhaps this is because journalists have not adequately recognized that they too are a part of the process of legislative representation and that they share in its moral meaning.

Notes

1. Michael J. O'Neill, "A Problem for the Republic—A Challenge for Editors," in *The Adversary Press* (St. Petersburg, Fla.: Modern Media Institute, 1983), p. 4.

2. *The Adversary Press*, p. viii.

3. Cf. Lloyd N. Cutler, "To Form a Government," *Foreign Affairs*, vol. 59: no. 1 (Fall, 1980):126–43; and Samuel P. Huntington, *American Politics and the Promise of Disharmony* (Cambridge, Mass.: Harvard University Press, 1981).

4. *The Adversary Press*, pp. 4; 12.

5. For general discussions of financial disclosure regulations in Congress see Congressional Quarterly, *Congressional Ethics*, 2d ed. (Washington, D. C.: Congressional Quarterly Press, 1980) and Joel L. Fleishman, "The Disclosure Model and Its Limitations," in *Revising the United States Senate Code of Ethics. A Hastings Center Report* Special Supplement (Hastings-on-Hudson, N. Y.: The Hastings Center, 1981), pp. 15–17.

6. For a detailed account of the page incident see United States Congress, House of Representatives, Committee on Standards of Official Conduct, *Report Pursuant to House Resolution 518*, 97th Congress, 2d session (Washington, D. C.: Government Printing Office, 1982).

7. Cf. Dennis F. Thompson, "The Private Lives of Public Officials," in *Public Duties: The Moral Obligations of Government Officials*, ed. by Joel L. Fleishman, Lance Liebman, and Mark H. Moore (Cambridge, Mass.: Harvard University Press, 1981), pp. 221–47.

8. The analysis in this section is drawn from Richard A. Schwarzlose, "Legislative Ethics and the Media: Historical Perspective," a paper presented to The Hastings Center Research Group on Legislative Ethics and the Media, June 2–3, 1983. On the history of American journalism and press-government relations see more generally see Frank Luther Mott, *American Journalism, A History: 1690–1960*, 3d ed. (New York: Macmillan Co., 1962); Edwin Emery and Michael Emery, *The Press in America: An Interpretive History of the Mass Media*, 4th ed. (Englewood Cliffs, N. J.: Prentice Hall, 1978); F. B. Marbut, *News from the Capitol: The Story of Washington Reporting* (Carbondale, Ill.: Southern Illinois University Press, 1971); and Culver H. Smith, *The Press, Politics, and Patronage: The American Government's Use of Newspapers, 1789–1875* (Athens, Ga.: University of Georgia Press, 1977).

9. Cf. Gerald Benjamin, ed., *The Communications Revolution in Politics* (New York: The Academy of Political Science, 1982); and Anne Haskell, "Live From Capitol Hill Where Politicians Use High Tech to Bypass the Press," *Washington Journalism Review* (November, 1982):48–50.

10. Cf. Stephen Hess, *The Washington Reporters* (Washington, D. C.: The Brookings Institution, 1981); Michael J. Robinson, "Three Faces of Congressional Media," in *The New Congress*, ed. by Thomas E. Mann and Norman J. Ornstein (Washington, D. C.: American Enterprise Institute, 1981), pp. 55–98; and Roger H. Davidson and Walter J. Oleszek, *Congress and Its Members* (Washington, D. C.: Congressional Quarterly Press, 1981), pp. 133–60.

11. For a more complete discussion of the issues raised in this section see *The Ethics of Legislative Life: A Report by The Hastings Center* (Hastings-on-Hudson, N. Y.: The Hastings Center, 1985).

12. Amy Gutmann and Dennis F. Thompson, "The Theory of Legislative Ethics," in *Representation and Responsibility: Exploring Legislative Ethics*, ed. by Bruce Jennings and Daniel Callahan (New York: Plenum Press, in press).

13. Keith S. Collins, ed., *Responsibility and Freedom in the Press, Are They in Conflict?* (Washington, D. C.: Citizen's Choice, Inc., 1985).

14. The Commission on Freedom of the Press, *A Free and Responsible Press* (Chicago, Ill.: University of Chicago Press, 1947). See also Zechariah Chafee, Jr., *Government and Mass Communications*, 2 vol. (Chicago, Ill.: University of Chicago Press, 1947); Fred S. Siebert, Theodore Peterson, and Wilbur Schramm, *Four Theories of the Press* (Urbana, Ill.: University of Illinois Press, 1979), pp. 73–104; and William L. Rivers, Wilbur Schramm and Clifford G. Christians, *Responsibility in Mass Communication*, 3d ed. (New York: Harper and Row, 1980).

15. Michael Schudson, "The News Media and the Democratic Process." A Wye Resource Paper (New York: Aspen Institute, 1983).

16. We are indebted to Stephen Bates, at present a student at Harvard Law School, who formulated these points in a background paper he prepared for a 1983 conference on Congress and the Media sponsored by the Institute of Politics at Harvard University and the *Los Angeles Times*.

Selected Bibliography

Abel, Elie, ed. *What's News*. San Francisco: Institute for Contemporary Studies, 1981.

Altheide, David L. *Creating Reality: How TV News Distorts Events*. Beverly Hills, Cal.: Sage, 1976.

Bagdikian, Ben H. *The Media Monopoly*. Boston: Beacon Press, 1983.

Balk, Alfred. *A Free and Responsive Press: The Twentieth Century Fund Task Force Report for a National News Council*. New York: The Twentieth Century Fund, Inc., 1973.

Blanchard, Robert O., ed. *Congress and the News Media*. New York: Hastings House, 1974.

The Ethics of Legislative Life. Hastings-on-Hudson, N.Y.: The Hastings Center, 1985.

Gans, Herbert J. *Deciding What's News: A Study of CBS Evening News, NBS Nightly News, Newsweek and Time*. New York: Pantheon Books, 1979.

Goodwin, H. Eugene. *Groping for Ethics in Journalism*. Ames: Iowa State University Press, 1983.

Graber, Doris. *Mass Media and American Politics*. Washington, D. C.: Congressional Quarterly Press, 1980.

Hulteng, John L. *The Messenger's Motives: Ethical Problems of the News Media*. Englewood Cliffs, N. J.: Prentice-Hall, 1976.

Hulteng, John L. *Playing It Straight: A Practical Discussion of the Ethical Principles of the American Society of Newspaper Editors*. Chester, Conn.: American Society of Newspaper Editors, 1981.

Lesher, Stephen. *Media Unbound: The Impact of Television Journalism on the Public*. Boston: Houghton Mifflin, 1982.

Mollenhoff, Clark R. *Investigative Reporting: From Courthouse to White House*. New York: Macmillan, 1981.

Purvis, Joyt H., ed. *The Press: Free and Responsible?* Austin, Tex.: The University of Texas, 1982.

Ranney, Austin. *Channels of Power: The Impact of Television on American Politics*. New York: Basic Books, 1983.

Rubin, Bernard, ed. *Questioning Media Ethics*. New York: Praeger Special Studies, 1978.

Schmul, Robert, ed. *The Responsibilities of Journalism*. Notre Dame, Ind.: Notre Dame Press, 1984.

Schudson, Michael. *Discovering the News*. New York: Basic Books, 1978.

Shaw, David. *Press Watch: A Provocative Look at How Newspapers Report the News*. New York: Macmillan, 1984.

Participants in the Legislative Ethics and the Media Project*

PROJECT CO-DIRECTORS

Daniel Callahan, Director, The Hastings Center

Bruce Jennings, Associate for Policy Studies, The Hastings Center

PROJECT CONSULTANTS

William Green, Vice President for University Relations, Duke University

Martin Linsky, Assistant Director, Institute of Politics, Harvard University

MEETING AND
INTERVIEW PARTICIPANTS

Irwin Arieff, *Legal Times of Washington*

Bill Arthur, *Charlotte Observer*

Joyce Bermel, Director of Public Information, The Hastings Center

William Brandon, Professor of Political Science, Seton Hall University

Daniel Callahan, Director, The Hastings Center

Lou Cannon, *The Washington Post*

Arthur L. Caplan, Associate for the Humanities, The Hastings Center

Deni T. Elliott, Institute of Politics, Harvard University

Alan Ehrenhalt, Congressional Quarterly, Inc.

Representative Barney Frank, United States House of Representatives

William Green, Vice President for University Relations, Duke University

William Greider, *Rolling Stone* Magazine

Amy Gutmann, Professor of Politics, Princeton University

Anne Haskell, Arlington, Virginia

Jay Hedlund, Common Cause

Senator Howell Heflin, United States Senate

Louis W. Hodges, Director, Society and the Professions Program, Washington and Lee University

Barry Hoffman, Westchester Rockland Newspapers

Milton Hoffman, Westchester Rockland Newspapers

Ellen Hume, *Wall Street Journal*

Brooks Jackson, *Wall Street Journal*

Bruce Jennings, Associate for Policy Studies, The Hastings Center

James C. Kirby, University of Tennessee College of Law

Martin Linsky, Assistant Director, Institute of Politics, Harvard University

Gayle McCracken, *Birmingham Post-Herald*

John Marttila, Marttila and Kiley, Boston, Massachusetts

Al May, *Raleigh News and Observer*

Vanessa Merton, C.U.N.Y. Law School at Queens College

S. J. Micciche, *The Boston Globe*

Frank Morring, *Scripps-Howard Newspapers*

Thomas Murray, University of Texas Medical Branch, Galveston, Texas

L. Richard Preyer, University of North Carolina, Chapel Hill; former U. S. Representative from North Carolina

John D. Saxon, Director, Corporate Issues, RCA Corporation; former Counsel, U. S. Senate Select Committee on Ethics

Richard Schwarzlose, Professor of Journalism, Northwestern University

Senator Paul Simon, United States Senate

Lauren Steele, Coca-Cola Company; former staff member, U. S. Senate

Robert M. Stern, General Counsel, California Commission on Campaign Financing; former General Counsel, California Fair Political Practices Commission

Dennis F. Thompson, Professor of Politics, Princeton University

Gregory Vlastos, Professor of Philosophy, University of California, Berkeley

Deborah Wadsworth, Executive Director, Smart Family Foundation; former Program Officer, John and Mary R. Markle Foundation

J. Jackson Walter, President, National Trust for Historic Preservation; former Director, U. S. Office of Government Ethics

Wallace Westfeldt, Lewisburg, W. Va.; former producer, NBC News

James G. Wieghart, *Scripps-Howard Newspapers*

Judy Woodruff, *MacNeil-Lehrer News Hour*

* Institutional affiliation for identification only

51

Authors

DANIEL CALLAHAN is Director of The Hastings Center. A philosopher and former executive editor of *Commonweal*, he is co-director of the Project on Legislative Ethics and the Media.

WILLIAM GREEN is Vice President for University Relations at Duke University. From 1980–81 he served as ombudsman for the *Washington Post*.

BRUCE JENNINGS, a political scientist, is Associate for Policy Studies at The Hastings Center and co-director of the Legislative Ethics and the Media Project.

MARTIN LINSKY is Assistant Director of the Institute of Politics, Harvard University. He has been an editorial writer for the *Boston Globe* and served in the Massachusetts state legislature from 1967–72.